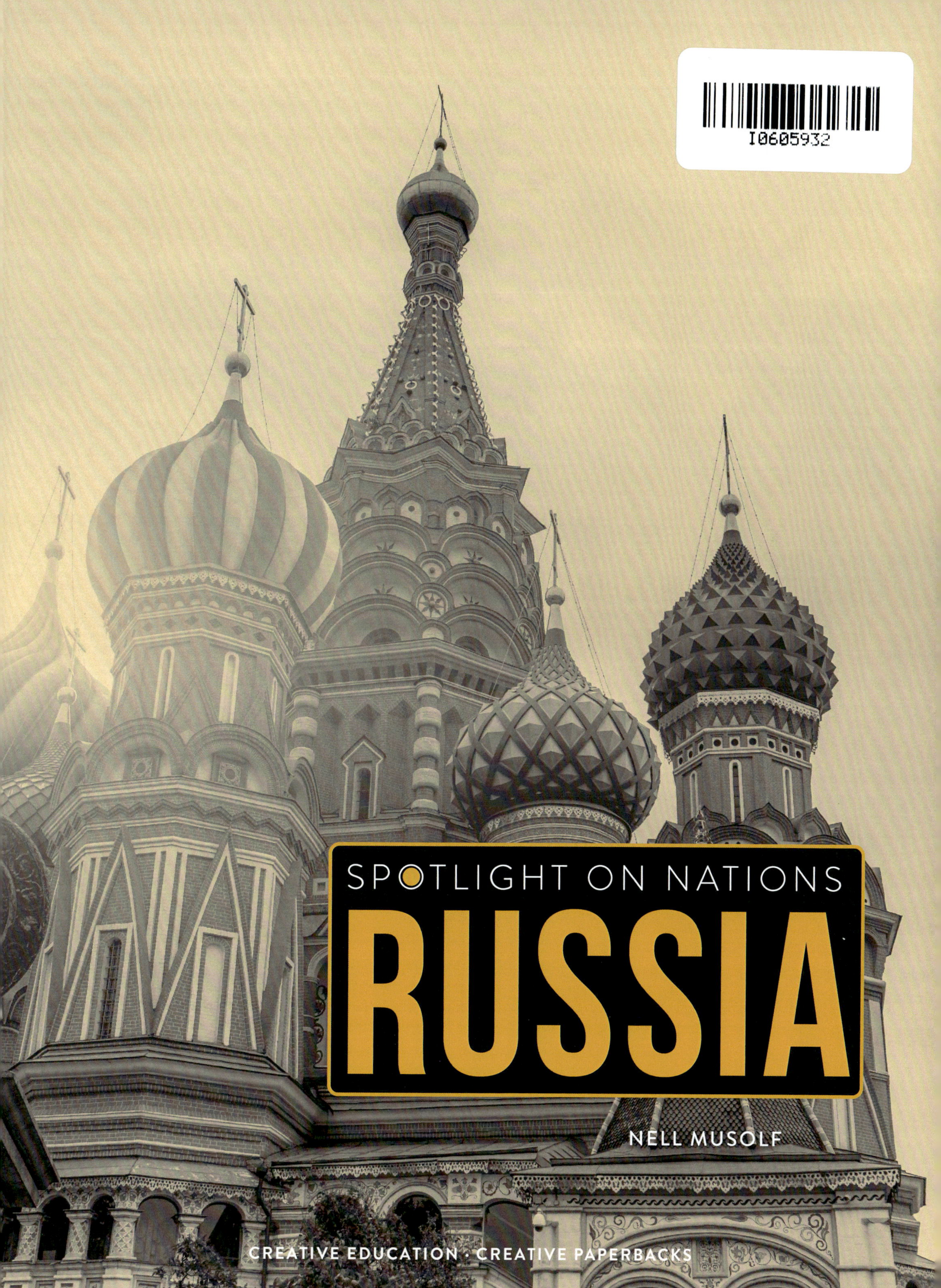

SPOTLIGHT ON NATIONS

RUSSIA

NELL MUSOLF

CREATIVE EDUCATION · CREATIVE PAPERBACKS

Published by Creative Education and Creative Paperbacks
P.O. Box 227, Mankato, Minnesota 56002
Creative Education and Creative Paperbacks are imprints of The Creative Company
www.thecreativecompany.us

Design and production by Blue Design, Inc.
Art direction by Tom Morgan
Edited by Ana Brauer

Photographs by Getty Images/Elena Liseykina, 4–5, Keystone-France, 18; Pexels/Evgeniy Zolotarev, 10, Yaroslav Shuraev, 28, Dmitry Trepolsky, 27; Unsplash/Christian Wiediger, cover, 1, Oleksandr Brovko, 26, Vladimir Fedotov, 9; Wikimedia Commons/Boevaya mashina, 15, Irving R. Wiles, 21, Jean-Marc Nattier, 11, Karel de Moor, 6, Kremlin.ru, 23, Miscellaneous Items in High Demand, PPOC, Library of Congress, 14, Pavel Zhukov, 29, Peter the Great, 8, 10, 14, 16, 20, 22, public domain, 16, Sergey Pesterev, 12, Theatre "Ballet" Moscow", 24, Zelma /Georgy Zelma, 17, Pavlov P., 3

Library of Congress Cataloging-in-Publication Data
Names: Musolf, Nell author
Title: Russia / by Nell Musolf.
Description: Mankato, Minnesota : Creative Education and Creative Paperbacks, [2026] | Series: Spotlight on nations | Includes bibliographical references and index. | Audience: Ages 10-13 | Audience: Grades 4–6 | Summary: "Explore Russia's geography, history, government, economy, cultural heritage, and modern challenges, plus its global influence and resilience. Written for middle-grade readers, this book includes timelines, sidebars, glossary, resources, and index"—Provided by publisher.
Identifiers: LCCN 2025017123 (print) | LCCN 2025017124 (ebook) | ISBN 9798895810743 library binding | ISBN 9798896800279 paperback | ISBN 9798895812006 ebook
Subjects: LCSH: Russia (Federation)—Juvenile literature
Classification: LCC DK510.56 .M87 2026 (print) | LCC DK510.56 (ebook) | DDC 947—dc23/eng/20250502
LC record available at https://lccn.loc.gov/2025017123
LC ebook record available at https://lccn.loc.gov/2025017124

Printed in the United States

CONTENTS

INTRODUCTION

LARGEST COUNTRY

Russia isn't just big. It is huge. Russia stretches over a large part of eastern Europe and northern Asia. It is the largest country in the world. Russia has many different environments. It has deserts and thick forests. Its land reaches up into the Arctic **tundra** to the north. To the south and east, Russia shares a border with 14 other countries. There are 11 time zones in Russia. Russia has the longest river in Europe, the Volga, and the largest lake, Ladoga.

Life has often been hard for people living in Russia. They have struggled with the harsh climate. The difference between the rich and the poor has caused tension in society. Russia was a monarchy before becoming **communist** in 1922. For much of the 20th century, Russia was one of the 15 **republics** that made up the Union of Soviet Socialist Republics (U.S.S.R.), or the Soviet Union. In 1991, Russia became an independent country when the Soviet Union dissolved. Russia has seen many changes in its history, and it will continue to see more changes in the future.

PETER THE GREAT

CLOSE-UP

Beard Tax

Peter the Great imposed a beard tax on the male citizens of Russia. He wanted to make Russian men look more European. The idea was not popular with the Orthodox Church, which saw facial hair as a sign of faithfulness.

CHAPTER ONE

RUSSIAN HISTORY

Humans have lived in what is now Russia for thousands of years. By the ninth century, Slavic people in Ukraine mixed with Scandinavians known as Varangians. Together, they were called the Rus. Their territory was called Kyivan Rus, and its capital was the town of Kyiv.

Mongols from Central Asia invaded Kyivan Rus in 1200. During the Mongol reign, Novgorod in western Russia and Moscow in the north became powerful states. The Mongols were defeated in 1480 by Ivan III (3), also known as Ivan the Great.

A ruler named Ivan IV (4) was Russia's first **tsar**. He ruled Russia from 1533 to 1584. Ivan IV removed the Mongols from Kiev and expanded Russian land. However, he ruled the people so harshly that he earned the nickname Ivan the Terrible.

Another important tsar was Peter the Great, who ruled for 42 years. Peter's goal was to make Russia modern and more like Europe. After Peter died in 1725, his wife Catherine became empress of Russia. She was the

MILESTONES IN RUSSIAN HISTORY

862

- Kievan Rus, the first major East Slavic State, is founded

1237–40

- Mongols invade Kyivan Rus and destroy Kyiv and Moscow

first woman to rule the country. Before her death in 1727, Catherine passed control to Peter's grandson, Peter II (2). Several other rulers had relatively short reigns until Catherine the Great came into power in 1762. Catherine the Great focused on improving country's arts and culture. Under her 34-year rule, Russia became modernized, and a large amount of land was added to the Russian Empire, including Crimea, Lithuania, and Ukraine.

CLOSE-UP

Forested

Russia has 643 billion trees, or one-fifth of the entire world's trees. Most of the trees are in the boreal forest, the world's largest land biome. The boreal forest was once completely covered by glaciers.

The 20th century saw the end of the monarchy. Tsar Nicholas II (2) was removed as leader in 1917. Vladimir Lenin, the leader of the **Bolsheviks**, became ruler. Under Lenin, the Russian Empire was organized into the Union of Soviet Socialist Republics (U.S.S.R.) or Soviet Union. Regions such as Ukraine and Belarus became Soviet republics.

Tsar Nicholas II

Russia's last tsar, Nicholas II (2) or Nikolai Romanov, is best remembered not for his reign as Russia's leader, but for how his life ended. After giving up the crown, the Romanovs were sent to Siberia, an area of Russia located in northern Asia. The Bolsheviks executed the entire family there in 1918. It wasn't until 1976 that the remains of most of the family members were found. In 1998, Tsar Nicholas II (2) and his family were given a state funeral. They were reburied in St. Petersburg. The skeletons of the final two members of the family were found and identified in 2007.

During World War II (1939–45), Russia was **allied** with the United States. After the war ended in 1945, the Cold War began between the two countries and their allies over the spread of communism. It was called a cold war because there were no military battles. Instead, fighting was done through political and economic actions. The Cold War ended in 1991 when the U.S.S.R. broke into 15 independent states. Russia is the largest of these states. That same year, Russia had its first presidential election, and Boris Yeltsin became president.

Yeltsin remained president until 1999. Vladimir Putin served as president from 2000 to 2008. He was reelected in 2012. Putin is a powerful leader who has not always been popular with the people of Russia. His decision to invade Ukraine in 2014 and again in 2022 has been criticized by some Russian citizens and by much of the rest of the world.

1480–1505

Ivan the Great rules, freeing Russia from the Mongols

1547–84

Ivan the Terrible rules, becoming the first tsar of Russia

CLOSE-UP

Catfest

The Hermitage Museum in St. Petersburg houses around 70 cats. Cats are believed to have been introduced there by Empress Elizabeth in 1745 to control the mice population. An annual holiday called "Catfest" celebrates the museum's cats and their role in its history.

HISTORICAL  HIGHLIGHT

War in Ukraine

Ukraine has been independent from Russia since 1991. At that time, a document was signed giving all nuclear weapons owned by Ukraine to Russia. In 2008, Ukraine asked to be part of the North Atlantic Treaty Organization (NATO). NATO is a military alliance formed after World War II and made up of 30 countries. Russia did not want Ukraine to be part of NATO since that would give Ukraine more military power. In 2014 and again in 2022, Russia invaded Ukraine, beginning a war between the two countries.

Catherine I was Russia's first FEMALE leader.

1689–1725

Peter the Great is ruler and builds a new capital in St. Petersburg

1762

Catherine the Great becomes Empress of Russia and adds territory while working to modernize the country

CLOSE-UP
Lake Baikal

Lake Baikal is located in Siberia. With a depth of 5,387 feet (1,642 meters), it is the deepest lake in the world and holds about 20 percent of the entire world's freshwater.

CHAPTER TWO

GOVERNMENT AND ECONOMY

Although Russia is an old country, its current government model is fairly new. Since 1993, Russia has been a federal semi-presidential republic with a president, a prime minister, and a cabinet. The president is elected by the people and chooses the prime minister and cabinet. The three offices share executive powers.

The Russian Constitution was adopted by the government in 1993 and revised in 2014. Russia is made up of 21 smaller republics, nine territories, 46 regions, and four districts. All of these are controlled by the government in Moscow, the capital of Russia.

Russia's economy is based on its many natural resources including gas, oil, and coal. Russia has more than 20 percent of the world's natural resources. Russia also has vast amounts of gold in the Ural Mountains and Siberia. Large tin and iron reserves can be found in Russia. Its thick forests help Russia provide wood for other parts of the world. Russia's biggest

1914

- Russia enters World War I

1917

- Russian Revolution ends the Romanov dynasty, and Vladimir Lenin takes control. The Soviet Union is established

CLOSE-UP

Keeping Time

When the Winter Palace was stormed by Bolsheviks, a clock in the palace stopped at the exact moment Russia became a communist country. On October 26, 1917, the clock stopped at 2:10 a.m. One hundred years later, the clock was restarted.

HISTORICAL HIGHLIGHT

Tough Tank

Russia has a tank called the T-14 Armata. This tank was first made in 2014. Since then, newer models have been built. What is so special about a T-14? For starters, it's big, weighing in at 55 tons (50 metric tons). It can also move up to 55 miles (88.5 kilometers) per hour. Its design keeps the crew below and away from the turret. The T-14 was designed to be a "super-tank" that would be almost impossible to blow up. However, the tank is very expensive to produce. Each one costs between 5 and 9 million US dollars to make.

exports are energy, metals, and high-tech military equipment. Russia exports wheat, barley, grains, peas, meat, and seafood to more than 160 countries.

Russia trades with other countries. Germany, Italy, the United States, and the United Kingdom are some of its trading partners. Most of Russia's exports are oil and petroleum products. Russia's gross domestic product (GDP) was approximately 8.4 trillion USD in 2024. The GDP of a country measures how healthy a country's economy is. Russia's GDP grew by 3.6 percent in 2023. This was the fastest growing economy in the world. But much of the growth was based on the war in Ukraine.

Because of the Ukraine war, Russia has been building more military equipment than it has in the past. However, the war has been costly for the country, too. Spending so much money on the military has caused the government to put off spending money on other projects, such as the **infrastructure**.

Russia's unemployment rate is currently low. Most people who want to work are able to find jobs. Most people work in the service industry. The service industry makes up about half the jobs in Russia. A service industry job might be working in a store, at a restaurant, or in customer service. Other jobs include equipment operators, manufacturing, and technology specialists.

T-14 TANK

1918

- Moscow becomes the capitol of Russia

1929

- Joseph Stalin becomes dictator of Russia

CLOSE-UP

Stalin

Joseph Stalin led the Soviet Union from 1924 until his death in 1953. He was a brutal leader and often had anyone who didn't agree with him killed. Under Stalin, an estimated 20 million Russians died from starvation, purges, or in slave labor camps.

HISTORICAL HIGHLIGHT

Power Move

Before Vladimir Putin backed changes to Russia's constitution, presidents could serve two consecutive four-year terms. Putin was president from 2000 to 2008, then became prime minister while Dmitry Medvedev served as president. Under Medvedev, presidential terms were extended to six years starting in 2012. Putin became president again that year. In 2020, a constitutional amendment reset Putin's term count, allowing him to remain president for two extra terms. Not all people were happy with the amendment. Some felt it was a power move on the president's part. Others were pleased to have Putin remain in power.

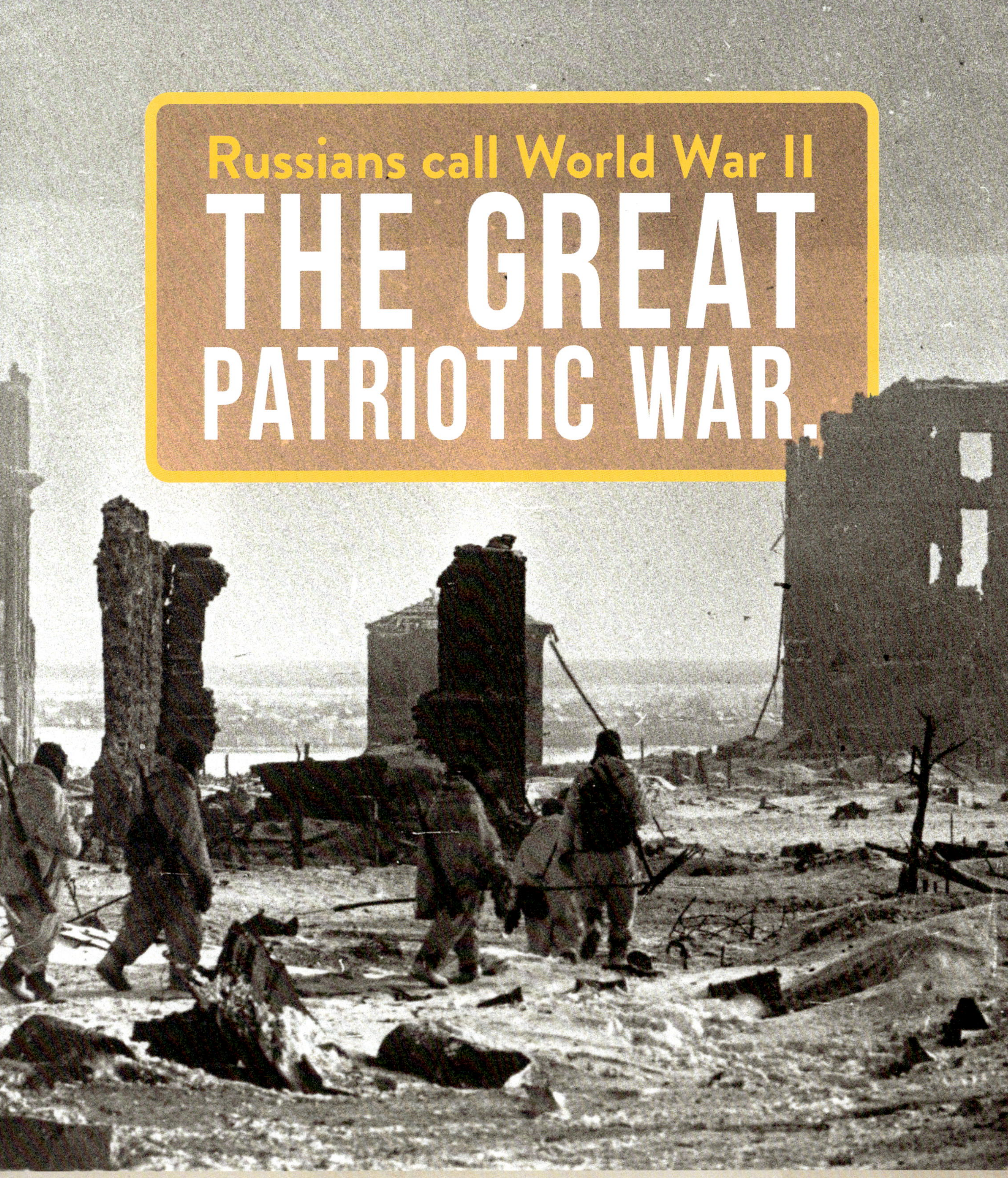

1939

World War II begins. Russia first aligns with Adolph Hitler but joins the Allies after Hitler breaks their agreement

1957

Sputnik I is launched, the first artificial satellite that orbits the earth

CLOSE-UP

Yuri Gagarin

In 1955, the Soviet Union and the U.S. competed in the Space Race. Each country wanted to lead in space exploration. The Soviets won the first round when Yuri Gagarin became the first human to orbit the earth on April 12, 1961.

CHAPTER THREE

PEOPLE, CULTURE, AND TRADITIONS

Russia has more than 120 different **ethnic** groups, and about 100 languages are spoken. Most people are Russian, but other ethnic groups include Ukrainians, Armenians, and Tatars. The majority of the population lives in cities. The rest live in rural areas. Most Russians live in western Russia. In cities, people usually live in apartments. In the country, people often live in houses.

Russian families tend to be close-knit and enjoy spending time together. Some urban families have country cottages called a ***dacha***. Holidays and weekends are often spent at the family dacha. Grandparents are called ***babushka*** (grandma) and ***dedushka*** (grandpa). They have a special relationship with their grandchildren and are treated with respect.

Russian parents are very involved with their children. Parents are protective and tend to make decisions without talking things over with their children. Children are expected to let their parents know where they are

1961

Soviet pilot Yuri Gagarin becomes the first person to fly in space

1985

Mikhail Gorbachev is elected general secretary of the Communist Party

at all times. When children are home, they often spend time with other family members talking and sharing what happened during their days.

Teenagers and young people spend their free time watching television, going to movies, and hanging out with friends. Popular sports are hockey, soccer, skiing, and volleyball. Another popular pastime is chess.

Russian men are required to join the military for at least one year after they turn 18. If an 18-year-old male is attending college, they still must have equivalent military training. Men and women can join the Russian Armed Forces. Some people join for financial reasons, and others join for patriotic reasons.

Education has three stages. They are primary, basic general, and secondary. Primary education starts at age six and continues four years. Basic general education lasts five years and is followed by two or three years

Spilling Tea

Tea is a staple of Russian culture and one of the country's most popular drinks. With its cold climate, a cup of hot tea helps warm people from the inside out. Tea is enjoyed all day long, from breakfast to bedtime. When someone invites a friend over for tea, it is usually an invitation to have a long, friendly talk. Drinking tea together is a Russian way to talk about problems and to share feelings in a comfortable environment. Teatime is often "we" time!

1986

- The Chernobyl disaster takes place at the Chernobyl Nuclear Power Plant in Ukraine

1991

- Boris Yeltsin wins Russia's first popular presidential election

of secondary education. After secondary education, students take an examination if they want to go on to higher education.

In the Russian culture, people usually eat three main meals a day, but meals don't have a set time. It's common to have tea or coffee between meals. Meals usually include meat, noodles, cabbage, and soup. A popular soup is borscht, which is made from beets and topped with sour cream. Pelmeni are dumplings filled with meat. Caviar is a treat for special occasions. Caviar is made from salt-cured eggs of sturgeon fish. It is eaten on crackers or as a topping on other dishes.

About half of the population are Eastern Orthodox Christians. Other faiths followed include Islam, Protestantism, and Judaism. About one-third of the population follows no religion.

CLOSE-UP

Putin

Before leading Russia, Vladimir Putin worked as a spy for the KGB during the 1980s. The KGB was the Soviet Union's secret spy agency. Putin's past shaped his leadership style.

HISTORICAL HIGHLIGHT

Chernobyl

On April 26, 1986, an accident happened at the Chernobyl Nuclear Power Plant in Ukraine, which was then part of the U.S.S.R. The explosion at Reactor 4 released radioactive particles into the air, causing illness and death among those exposed to high radiation. Thousands of people were forced to leave their homes. Radioactive contamination spread across Europe, reaching as far as Italy. Crops and livestock were affected for hundreds of miles (kilometers). At first, the Soviet government tried to hide what happened, but it was impossible. Stricter safety rules were introduced after the disaster.

2000	2020	2022
Vladimir Putin is elected president	A referendum allowing Putting to remain in power is passed	Russia invades Ukraine

CHAPTER FOUR

MODERN-DAY RUSSIA

Russia has always held a central place in the world. As the world's largest country, Russia takes up one-tenth of the world's **landmass**. It has vast amounts of natural resources that help fuel other countries. The wheat grown in Russia feeds people around the world. Russia has produced some of the greatest artists in history including writer Leo Tolstoy and ballet dancer Rudolf Nureyev.

Russia's past helps explain what life is like there today. For hundreds of years, Russia was ruled by powerful tsars. Most people in Russia lived in poverty, while a small group had lavish lifestyles. After the Russian Revolution of 1917, people were hopeful that their lifestyles would improve. It wasn't until the 1980s that the average Russian citizen began to see real change in their country.

In 1985, President Mikhail Gorbachev introduced ***perestroika***, which means "restructuring." This policy aimed to change the Soviet economy by allowing some private business ownership and reducing government control. As a result, Russians began to have slightly easier lives. Gorbachev soon followed with ***glasnost***, meaning "openness," which encouraged more

CLOSE-UP

Railway

The longest railway in the world is in Russia. The Trans-Siberian Railway travels from Moscow to Vladivostok, a trip that takes around six days. The railway is 5,771 miles (9,288 km) long.

freedom of speech. For the first time in decades, people could discuss problems with their country without fear of punishment. These changes helped shape modern Russia and gave people more control of their lives.

The U.S.S.R. fell in 1991, and Russia became its own country again. Becoming Russia was not an easy change. Economic problems, environmental problems including the worst nuclear accident in history at Chernobyl, and two wars with Ukraine have been some of Russia's more recent struggles.

Today, most people living in Russia are satisfied with the freedoms they have. While many people would like to see more freedom in the media, Russians are hopeful about the future of their country. They feel safer than they have before and believe their standard of living has improved.

Because Russia is remote and not always accessible, the country has often seemed mysterious to the rest of the world. The history of Russia has shown that its people are strong. They grow up knowing how to battle a harsh physical environment. They learn how to take care of themselves at an early age with the help of their families. Most Russians are fiercely loyal to their country and want to see it grow and improve.

ALL ABOUT

RUSSIA

Continents: Europe and Asia

Capital city: Moscow

Population: 145 million

Official Language: Russian

Type of government: Federal semi-presidential republic

Currency: Ruble

VLADIMIR LENIN

Main religion practiced: Russian Orthodox

Colors on flag: White, blue, red

National flower: Chamomile

WORDS to Know

ally a person, group, or country that has joined with another for a particular purpose

Bolshevik a member of an extremist wing of the Russian Social Democratic Labour Party that seized power in 1917

communist a type of government and economic system in which goods are owned in common and available to all as needed

contaminate to soil or infect by contact or association

ethnic relating to a group of people who share the same culture, race, or nationality

infrastructure the basic physical systems that support a region

landmass a large body of land

republic form of government in which a country is ruled by representatives of the citizen body

tundra one of the huge plains in the arctic regions of North America, Europe, and Asia

tsar the title of male Russian rulers before 1917

LEARN MORE

Books

Blohm, Craig E. *Unprovoked War: Russia's Invasion of Ukraine*. San Diego: ReferencePoint Press, 2023.

Dickmann, Nancy. *Radiation Disaster!: Chernobyl, 1986*. Minneapolis: Bearport Publishing, 2023.

Walker, Tracy Sue. *Spotlight on Russia*. Minneapolis: Lerner Publications, 2024.

Websites

"Russia." Globe Trottin' Kids.

https://www.globetrottinkids.com/countries/russia/

"Russia Facts." National Geographic Kids.

https://www.natgeokids.com/uk/discover/geography/countries/russia-facts/

"Russia Facts for Kids." Kids World Travel Guide.

https://www.kids-world-travel-guide.com/russia-facts.html#google_vignette

Documentaries

Celinski, Andrzej, Polak, Hanna, dirs. *The Children of Leningradsky*. New York City, New York, HBO/Cinemax, 2005.

Langemann, Irene, dir. *Russia's Millennium Children*. Bonn, Germany, Deutsche Welle, 2019.

Lee, Alice, dir. *Russia – A Thousand Years of History*. United Kingdom, Lambent Productions, 2021.

Note: Every effort has been made to ensure that any websites listed above were active at the time of publication. However, because of the nature of the Internet, it is impossible to guarantee that these sites will remain active indefinitely or that their contents will not be altered.

Visit

THE KREMLIN

Visit the Kremlin, a historic fortress and the heart of Russia's government. This famous site includes palaces, cathedrals, and the president's official residence.

Moscow, Russia, 103132

ST. BASIL'S CATHEDRAL

Built by Ivan the Terrible in the 1550s, St. Basil's Cathedral is known for its colorful domes. Each dome tops one of nine separate chapels.

Red Square 7, Moscow, Russia, 109012

PETERHOF PALACE

Built by Peter the Great, this estate features beautiful gardens, fountains, and royal buildings. It's often called the "Russian Versailles."

Razvodnaya Ulitsa, 2
Saint Petersburg, Russia, 198516

STATE HERMITAGE MUSEUM

Explore one of the largest and oldest museums in the world. Founded in 1764, it holds millions of art pieces and artifacts from around the globe.

Palace Square, 2, St Petersburg, Russia, 190000

INDEX